FIRST F

LATIN

Latin Grammar, Year One

Quizzes & Tests

Cheryl Lowe

MEMORIA PRESS

www.MemoriaPress.com

FIRST FORM LATIN
Latin Grammar, Year One

QUIZZES & TESTS
Cheryl Lowe
Contributing editors: Michael Simpson & Highlands Latin School faculty

ISBN 978-1-61538-843-1

Cover illustration: The women of Rome plead with Coriolanus

Table of Contents

Grading

The following are *suggestions* only. Feel free to modify them according to the needs of your student(s).

- **Vocabulary:** 2 points when students must include the principal parts (verbs), the genitive singular and gender (nouns), or multiple nominative forms/endings (adjectives and many pronouns). 1 point for all other parts of speech (adverbs, prepositions, conjunctions, and interjections).
    - » **Note:** Deduct 0.5 points if a student omits or incorrectly gives any cases, prepositions, or constructions that the word takes, e.g., w/gen., w/**ad**, w/infin. (applies to *Second Form Latin* and above)
- **Declensions & Conjugations:** 1 point per blank: 0.5 for the stem and 0.5 for the ending. If the student consistently used the wrong *stem* but wrote the correct *endings*, consider weighting the stem 0.25 points and the endings 0.75.
- **Fill in the Blank/Grammar:** 1 point per blank.
- **Form Drills:** 1 point per form: 0.25 points each for the word, stem, tense/case, and ending.
- **Translation:** Do not be too harsh on this section; mastery of forms and vocabulary is most important. Use a scale of 0-2 points for shorter sentences (two to four *Latin* words) and 0-3 points for longer sentences (five or more *Latin* words). Give partial points for *any* correct words and/or forms. Reserve 0 for answers that are left blank or completely wrong.
    - » **Note:** For English to Latin translations, assign points based on the length of the answer in the Key, but grade even more leniently than you would a Latin to English translation.
- ***New* Latin Sayings:** 2 points if completely correct, 1 point if there are only a few minor mistakes, and no points if left blank or completely wrong. ***Review* Latin Sayings:** 1 point per saying.

For the **final grade**, divide the points earned by the points possible, round to the nearest hundred or thousand, then multiply by 100 to get a final percentage. For example:

27 points earned / 31 points possible = 0.8709
0.87 x 100 = 87.0% or 0.875 x 100 = 87.5%

Parsing and Labeling Key

When completing Form Drills or Translations, students should first **parse** each word, i.e., give its grammatical attributes and translation by answering the parsing prompts. Students should also **label** the function of each word in sentences of two or more words. *First Form Latin* will gradually introduce the following parsing prompts, parsing answers, and function labels:

Parsing Prompts

- Case (abbreviation: C)
- Conjugation (Cj)
- Declension (D)
- Gender (G)
- Number (N)
- Person (P)
- Tense (T)
- Translation (Tr)

Parsing Answers

- ***Case:*** nominative (nom.), genitive (gen.), dative (dat.), accusative (acc.), ablative (abl.)
- ***Conjugation:*** 1st, 2nd, irregular (ir)
- ***Declension:*** 1st, 2nd, 3rd, 4th, 5th
- ***Gender:*** masculine (m.), feminine (f.), neuter (n.)
- ***Person:*** 1st, 2nd, 3rd
- ***Number:*** singular (S), plural (P)
- ***Tense:*** present (pres.), imperfect (impf.), future (fut.), perfect (perf.), pluperfect (plupf.), future perfect (fut. pf.)
- ***Translation:*** he, she, it (hsi)

Function Labels

- Adj *for Adjective*
- Adv *for Adverb*
- CI *for Complementary Infinitive*
- DO *for Direct Object*
- LV *for Linking Verb*
- PA *for Predicate Adjective*
- PrN *for Predicate Nominative*
- S *for Subject*
- V *for Verb*

Translation Checklist

As sentences become more complex, students are often insecure about their answers and want confirmation for every choice they make. Students need to learn how to evaluate their answers correctly, so they don't waste class time asking about every deviation from the key. Below is a checklist to help students distinguish between an error and legitimate choices in their answers. Go over this with your students thoroughly. These topics are listed in the order that students will encounter them, so you will have to refer to this checklist throughout the year.

1. **Word Choice.** There are two or more meanings for many vocabulary words. All choices are correct unless there are specific restrictions about certain meanings. The answer key doesn't always give each alternative meaning. Sometimes the key will give both choices for words with more than one meaning, but not on a consistent basis.
2. **Word Order.** Latin word order is very flexible, so an answer that deviates from the norm is not wrong. However, the exercises stick with the usual word order *most of the time*, and so should the student.
3. **Verb Tenses**
   - **a.** There are three choices for the present tense.
     I call *I do call* *I am calling*
   - **b.** There are three choices for the perfect tense.
     I called *I did call* *I have called*

Lesson 1 Quiz

Name ______________________ Date __________

A. Vocabulary & Latin Saying: Give the Latin for each vocabulary word.

1. I call ____________
2. I carry ____________
3. I give ____________
4. I guard, keep ____________
5. I love, like ____________
6. I prepare ____________
7. I beg, pray ____________
8. I stand ____________
9. I swim ____________
10. I wash ____________

Saying: Let us recite together. ____________

Derivative: People often ____________ money to charities.

B. Grammar Questions

1. Verb families are called ____________.
2. Latin is a language of ____________ and ____________.

   The ____________ is the part of the word that doesn't change.

C. Conjugate the verb porto in the present tense with meanings.

present stem: ____________

Person	LATIN		ENGLISH MEANINGS	
	Singular	Plural	Singular	Plural
1st				
2nd				
3rd				

D. Form Drills: Circle tense ending (#1), parse, then translate.

1. vocamus

Person: ____________

Number: ____________

Translation: ____________

2. he washes

Person: ____________

Number: ____________

Translation: ____________

E. Bonus

Give an English example of: the simple present ____________

the progressive present ____________

and the emphatic present ____________

Lesson 2 Quiz

Name ______________________ Date __________

A. Vocabulary & Latin Saying: Give the Latin for each vocabulary word.

1. I desire, wish ______________
2. I err, wander ______________
3. I fight ______________
4. I help ______________
5. I look at ______________
6. I plow ______________
7. I praise ______________
8. I shout ______________
9. I tell ______________
10. I tempt ______________

Saying: The Mother Was Standing ______________

Derivative: A person who tells a story is a ______________.

B. Grammar Questions

1. In Latin grammar, *imperfect* means ______________.
2. How many words are necessary to make a Latin sentence? ______________

C. Conjugate the verb clamo in the present and imperfect tenses.

present stem: ______________

Person	PRESENT		IMPERFECT	
	Singular	Plural	Singular	Plural
1st				
2nd				
3rd				

D. Form Drills: Circle tense ending (#1) or box any helping verbs (#2), parse, then translate.

1. optabant

Person: ________ *Number:* ________

Tense: ______________

Translation: ______________

2. you were praising

Person: ________ *Number:* ________

Tense: ______________

Translation: ______________

E. Bonus: Circle tense ending, parse, then translate.

1. pugnatis

Person: ________ *Number:* ________

Tense: ______________

Translation: ______________

Lesson 3 Quiz Name________________________ Date__________

A. Vocabulary & Latin Saying: Give the Latin for each vocabulary word.

1. I adore ______________________
2. I greet______________________
3. I judge, consider ______________________
4. I live in, dwell______________________
5. I overcome, surpass ______________________
6. I sail ______________________
7. I seize______________________
8. I set free______________________
9. I walk______________________
10. I work______________________

Saying: Then we will fight in the shade. ______________________

Derivative: A vehicle that carries sick or injured people to a hospital is an______________________.

B. Grammar Question

1. The two basic parts of a sentence are the______________________.

C. Conjugate the verb **laboro** in the present, imperfect, and future tenses.

present stem: ______________________

Person	Present		Imperfect	
1st				
2nd				
3rd				

Future	

D. Form Drills: Circle tense ending (#1) or box any helping verbs (#2), parse, then translate.

1. navigabo	**2.** they will adore
Person: __________ *Number:* __________	*Person:* __________ *Number:* __________
Tense: ______________________	*Tense:* ______________________
Translation: ______________________	*Translation:* ______________________

E. Bonus

Derivative: Patrick Henry said, "Give me ______________________ or give me death."

Lesson 4 Review Quiz

Name________________________________ Date____________

A. Vocabulary: Give the *infinitive* of each vocabulary word.

1. to desire, wish ____________________
2. to err, wander ____________________
3. to fight ____________________
4. to give ____________________
5. to guard, keep ____________________
6. to praise ____________________
7. to sail ____________________
8. to swim ____________________
9. to tell ____________________
10. to work ____________________

B. Grammar Questions

Choose the correct answer from the word bank.

-are	future	imperfect	infinitive	present	principal parts	**re**	stems

1. The four main forms for each verb are called the verb's ____________________.
2. These forms provide the ____________________ needed to conjugate each verb in all its tenses.
3. The 2nd principal part is the ____________________ .
4. The 2nd principal part of every 1st conjugation verb ends in ____________________.
5. The official way to find the stem of a 1st conjugation verb is to drop the ____________ from the infinitive form.
6. The three tenses (in order) that make up the present system are ____________________, ____________________, and ____________________.

C. Conjugate the verb **lavo** in the present, imperfect, and future tenses.

present stem: ____________________

Person	Present		Imperfect	
1st				
2nd				
3rd				

Future	

D. Form Drills

Circle tense endings (#1-2) or box any helping verbs (#3-4), parse, then translate.

1. spectabunt *Person:* ________ *Number:* ________ *Tense:* ________ *Translation:* ________	**3.** we were praying *Person:* ________ *Number:* ________ *Tense:* ________ *Translation:* ________
2. líberas *Person:* ________ *Number:* ________ *Tense:* ________ *Translation:* ________	**4.** she will prepare *Person:* ________ *Number:* ________ *Tense:* ________ *Translation:* ________

E. Bonus: Latin Sayings

1. Stabat Mater ________________________________
2. In umbrā, ígitur, pugnábimus.________________________________

Lesson 5 Quiz

Name ____________________ Date __________

A. Latin Saying

I am a Roman citizen. ______________________________

B. Grammar Questions

1. The *to be* verb shows ____________________, not ____________________.
2. The first two principal parts of the *to be* verb in Latin are ____________________.

C. Conjugate the verb sum in the present, imperfect, and future tenses.

present stem: n/a

P	Present		Imperfect		Future	
1						
2						
3						

D. Form Drills: Box any helping verbs (#4-6), parse, then translate.

1. érimus *Person:* ________ *Number:* ________ *Tense:* ________ *Translation:* ________	**4.** they are *Person:* ________ *Number:* ________ *Tense:* ________ *Translation:* ________
2. erat *Person:* ________ *Number:* ________ *Tense:* ________ *Translation:* ________	**5.** I will be *Person:* ________ *Number:* ________ *Tense:* ________ *Translation:* ________
3. estis *Person:* ________ *Number:* ________ *Tense:* ________ *Translation:* ________	**6.** you (p) were *Person:* ________ *Number:* ________ *Tense:* ________ *Translation:* ________

E. Bonus

1. Are the personal endings of **sum** regular or irregular? ____________________
2. Is the infinitive of **sum** regular or irregular? ____________________

Lesson 6 Test: Unit I Name ______________________ Date __________

A. Vocabulary: Give the *infinitive* of each vocabulary word.

1. to adore ______________
2. to beg, pray ______________
3. to call ______________
4. to carry ______________
5. to desire, wish ______________
6. to err, wander ______________
7. to fight ______________
8. to give ______________
9. to greet ______________
10. to guard, keep ______________
11. to help ______________
12. to judge, consider ______________
13. to live in, dwell ______________
14. to look at ______________
15. to love, like ______________
16. to overcome, surpass ______________
17. to plow ______________
18. to praise ______________
19. to prepare ______________
20. to sail ______________
21. to seize ______________
22. to set free ______________
23. to shout ______________
24. to stand ______________
25. to swim ______________
26. to tell ______________
27. to tempt ______________
28. to walk ______________
29. to wash ______________
30. to work ______________

B. Latin Sayings

1. In choro recitemus. ______________
2. Civis Romanus sum. ______________
3. Stabat Mater ______________
4. In umbrā, ígitur, pugnábimus. ______________

C. Grammar Questions

1. Verb families are called ______________ .
2. The six attributes of a Latin verb are ______________
______________ .
3. Latin is a language of ______________ and ______________ .
The ______________ is the part of the word that doesn't change.
4. Give the three tenses that make up the present system. ______________
____
5. The forms that provide the stems needed to conjugate a verb in all its tenses are called the
______________ ______________ .
6. What is the name of the second of these forms? ______________
7. The infinitive of every 1st conjugation verb ends in ______________ .

C. Grammar Questions, continued

8. In English, *I call* is the ________________ present, *I am calling* is the ______________________ present, and *I do call* is the ________________________ present.
9. The two basic parts of a sentence are the ____.
10. How many words are necessary to make a Latin sentence? ______________________________
11. The *to be* verb shows ______________________________, not ________________________.
12. Give the English forms of the *to be* verb. ____

____

D. Conjugate the verb **voco** in the present, imperfect, and future tenses.

first two principal parts: ______________________________ present stem: ____________

P	Present		Imperfect	
1				
2				
3				

Future	

E. Conjugate the verb **sum** in the present, imperfect, and future tenses.

first two principal parts: ______________________________ present stem: n/a

P	Present		Imperfect	
1				
2				
3				

Future	

F. Form Drills

Circle tense endings (#1-3) or box any helping verbs (#4-6), parse, then translate.

1. salutabamus *Person:* ________ *Number:* ________ *Tense:* ________ *Translation:* ________	**4.** they will tell *Person:* ________ *Number:* ________ *Tense:* ________ *Translation:* ________
2. natabit *Person:* ________ *Number:* ________ *Tense:* ________ *Translation:* ________	**5.** you (p) were adoring *Person:* ________ *Number:* ________ *Tense:* ________ *Translation:* ________
3. júdicas *Person:* ________ *Number:* ________ *Tense:* ________ *Translation:* ________	**6.** they are *Person:* ________ *Number:* ________ *Tense:* ________ *Translation:* ________

G. Bonus

The answers will be derivatives of the following Latin words.

amo	aro	hábito	servo	specto

1. Land that can be plowed for growing crops is ________________.
2. A person who does an activity for the love of it rather than for a salary is an________________.
3. The natural environment of a plant or animal is its________________.
4. Many people today are very dedicated to the ________________ of wildlife, land, and other natural resources.
5. To look at something closely for flaws is to ________________.

Lesson 7 Quiz

Name________________________________ Date_____________

A. Vocabulary & Latin Saying: Give the *principal parts* of the following verbs.

1st	2nd	3rd	4th
clamo			
do			
specto			
pugno			
lavo			
sto			
óccupo			
narro			

Latin Saying: To err is human. ____

B. Grammar Questions

1. What is the name of the 2nd principal part? ____
2. A complementary infinitive ________________________________ the action of the main verb.

C. Translation

Parse and label, then translate. Remember to underline any complementary infinitives.

Parsing Abbreviations & Function Labels

Abbreviations: ***Person*** = *1, 2, 3;* ***Number*** = *S, P;* ***Tense*** = *pres., impf., fut.;* ***Translation:*** *hsi* (for *he/she/it*).

Labels: ***Subject*** = *S,* ***Verb*** = *V,* ***Complementary Infinitive*** = *CI.*

Parsing Prompts Key: ***P*** = Person, ***N*** = Number, ***T*** = Tense, ***Tr*** = Translation

1. Optat | **juvare.**

*P:*____*N:*____*T:*______________ | *Tr:*__________________

*Tr:*____

Final Tr:____

D. Bonus: Parse and label, then translate.

1. Navigare | **parabamus.**

*Tr:*____________________ | *P:*____*N:*____*T:*______________

*Tr:*____

Final Tr:____

Lesson 8 Quiz

Name ______________________ Date __________

A. Vocabulary & Latin Saying: Give the Latin for each vocabulary word.

1. always ______________________
2. ever ______________________
3. never ______________________
4. not ______________________
5. now ______________________
6. often ______________________
7. then, at that time ______________________
8. today ______________________
9. tomorrow ______________________
10. yesterday ______________________

Latin Saying: now or never ______________________

B. Grammar Questions

1. In Latin grammar, *perfect* means ______________________ and *imperfect* means ______________________ .
2. Three helping verbs that may be used with the perfect tense are ______________________.

C. Conjugate the following verbs in the perfect tense.

principal parts of **pugno**: ______________________ perf. stem: __________

principal parts of **sto**: ______________________ perf. stem: __________

P	PERFECT (pugno)		PERFECT (sto)	
1				
2				
3				

D. Form Drills: Circle tense ending (#1) or box any helping verbs (#2), parse, then translate.

Prompts Key: ***P*** = Person, ***N*** = Number, ***T*** = Tense, ***Tr*** = Translation

1. salutavisti

P: __________ *N:* __________

T: ______________________

Tr: ______________________

2. he has carried

P: __________ *N:* __________

T: ______________________

Tr: ______________________

E. Bonus: Parse and label, then translate.

1. Numquam

Tr: ______________________

aravi.

P: ____ *N:* ____ *T:* __________

Tr: ______________________

Final Tr: ______________________

Lesson 9 Quiz

Name______________________ Date__________

A. Vocabulary & Latin Saying: Give the *infinitive* of each vocabulary word.

1. to accuse ______________________
2. to ask ______________________
3. to change ______________________
4. to deny ______________________
5. to disturb ______________________
6. to doubt ______________________
7. to fly ______________________
8. to hide ______________________
9. to hope ______________________
10. to think ______________________

Derivative: The opposite of *positive* is ______________________.

Latin Saying: always faithful ______________________

B. Grammar Questions

1. The pluperfect tense endings are identical to the ______________ tense of ______________.
2. The pluperfect tense describes a ______________ action completed prior to another ______________ action.

C. Conjugate the verb **volo** in the perfect and pluperfect tenses.

principal parts: ______________________ perf. stem: __________

P	Perfect		Pluperfect	
1				
2				
3				

D. Form Drills: Circle tense ending (#1) or box any helping verbs (#2), parse, then translate.

Prompts Key: ***P*** = Person, ***N*** = Number, ***T*** = Tense, ***Tr*** = Translation

1. rogáverat

P: __________ *N:* __________

T: ______________________

Tr: ______________________

2. we had hidden

P: __________ *N:* __________

T: ______________________

Tr: ______________________

E. Bonus: Parse and label, then translate.

1. Speráverant

*P:*____*N:*____*T:*__________

*Tr:*______________________

laborare.

*Tr:*______________________

Final Tr:______________________

Lesson 10 Quiz

Name ______________________ Date __________

A. Vocabulary & Latin Saying: Give the *infinitive* of each vocabulary word.

1. to address ______________________
2. to attack ______________________
3. to blame ______________________
4. to create ______________________
5. to delight, please ______________________
6. to explore ______________________
7. to report ______________________
8. to show, point out ______________________
9. to wait for, expect ______________________
10. to wound ______________________

Derivative: The area where you are ______________________ is your Achilles' heel.

Latin Saying: Fortune aids the brave. ______________________

B. Grammar Questions

1. The future perfect tense endings are *almost* the same as the ______________ tense of **sum**.
2. The future perfect tense describes a ______________ action that will be completed prior to another ______________ action.

C. Conjugate the verb **creo** in the perfect, pluperfect, and future perfect tenses.

principal parts: ______________________ perf. stem: __________

P	Perfect		Pluperfect	
1				
2				
3				

Future Perfect	

D. Form Drills: Circle tense ending (#1) or box any helping verbs (#2), parse, then translate.

Prompts Key: ***P*** = Person, ***N*** = Number, ***T*** = Tense, ***Tr*** = Translation

1. vulneráverit	**2.** they will have blamed
P: __________ *N:* __________	*P:* __________ *N:* __________
T: ______________________	*T:* ______________________
Tr: ______________________	*Tr:* ______________________

E. Bonus: Translate. Use the reverse side to parse if necessary.

1. we had attacked ______________________
2. you (p) had shown ______________________

Lesson 11 Quiz   Name ______________________ Date __________

A. Latin Saying

Pray and work. ____

B. Grammar Question

1. The *to be* verb shows ______________________, not ______________________.

C. Conjugate the verb **sum** in the perfect, pluperfect, and future perfect tenses.

principal parts: ______________________________ perf. stem: __________

Perfect		Pluperfect		Future Perfect	

D. Form Drills

Circle tense endings (#1-3) or box any helping verbs (#4-6), parse, then translate.

PROMPTS KEY: ***P*** = Person, ***N*** = Number, ***T*** = Tense, ***Tr*** = Translation

1. fuerunt *P:* __________ *N:* __________ *T:* ____________________ *Tr:* ____________________	**4.** you will have been *P:* __________ *N:* __________ *T:* ____________________ *Tr:* ____________________
2. fúeram *P:* __________ *N:* __________ *T:* ____________________ *Tr:* ____________________	**5.** she has been *P:* __________ *N:* __________ *T:* ____________________ *Tr:* ____________________
3. fuéritis *P:* __________ *N:* __________ *T:* ____________________ *Tr:* ____________________	**6.** he had been *P:* __________ *N:* __________ *T:* ____________________ *Tr:* ____________________

E. Bonus

1. Is the *infinitive* of **sum** regular or irregular? ______________________
2. Is the *present stem* of **sum** regular or irregular? ______________________
3. Is the *perfect stem* of **sum** regular or irregular? ______________________

Lesson 12 Test: Unit II

Name ______________________ Date __________

A. Vocabulary: For verbs, give the *infinitive* form.

1. to accuse ______________________
2. to address ______________________
3. to ask ______________________
4. to attack ______________________
5. to blame ______________________
6. to change ______________________
7. to create ______________________
8. to delight, please ______________________
9. to deny ______________________
10. to disturb ______________________
11. to doubt ______________________
12. to explore ______________________
13. to fly ______________________
14. to hide ______________________
15. to hope ______________________
16. to report ______________________
17. to show, point out ______________________
18. to think ______________________
19. to wait for, expect ______________________
20. to wound ______________________
21. always ______________________
22. ever ______________________
23. never ______________________
24. not ______________________
25. now ______________________
26. often ______________________
27. then, at that time ______________________
28. today ______________________
29. tomorrow ______________________
30. yesterday ______________________

B. Latin Sayings

1. Errare est humanum. ______________________
2. Fortes fortuna juvat. ______________________
3. nunc aut numquam ______________________
4. Ora et labora. ______________________
5. semper fidelis ______________________

C. Principal Parts: Complete the chart.

1st	2nd	3rd	4th
amo			
do			
juvo			
lavo			
sto			
sum			

D. Grammar Questions

1. Give the three tenses that make up the perfect system. ______________________________

   ____

2. How do you find the perfect stem? ____

3. In Latin grammar, *perfect* means ____________________________ and *imperfect* means

   ____________________________________ .

4. The pluperfect tense describes a ________________________ action completed prior to another

   ______________________ action.

5. The future perfect tense describes a ______________________ action that will be completed

   prior to another _________________________ action.

6. **Sum** is a ____________________________________ verb that shows

   ____________________________ , not _________________________ .

7. A complementary infinitive ____________________________ the action of the main verb.

E. Conjugate the verbs **celo** and **sum** in the perfect, pluperfect, and future perfect tenses.

principal parts: ____ perf. stem: __________

P	Perfect		Pluperfect	
1	*		**	
2				
3				

P	Future Perfect	
1	***	
2		
3		

**Translation:* ______________________________

***Translation:* ______________________________

****Translation:* ______________________________

principal parts: ____ perf. stem: __________

P	Perfect		Pluperfect	
1	*		**	
2				
3				

P	Future Perfect	
1	***	
2		
3		

**Translation:* ______________________________

***Translation:* ______________________________

****Translation:* ______________________________

F. Form Drills

Circle tense endings (#1-2) or box any helping verbs (#3-4), parse, then translate.

Prompts Key: *P* = Person, ***N*** = Number, ***T*** = Tense, ***Tr*** = Translation

1. appelláveram *P:* ______ *N:* ______ *T:* ______ *Tr:* ______	**3.** he will have denied *P:* ______ *N:* ______ *T:* ______ *Tr:* ______
2. fuit *P:* ______ *N:* ______ *T:* ______ *Tr:* ______	**4.** you (p) have explored *P:* ______ *N:* ______ *T:* ______ *Tr:* ______

G. Translation: Parse and label, then translate.

1. Demonstrare *Tr:* ______	**paráveras.** *P:*___ *N:*___ *T:*______ *Tr:* ______

Final Tr: ______

H. Bonus: Parse and label, then translate.

1. Non *Tr:* ______	**optaverunt** *P:*___ *N:*___ *T:*______ *Tr:* ______	**perturbare.** *Tr:* ______

Final Tr: ______

Lesson 13 Test: Units I & II

Name________________________________ Date______________

A. Vocabulary: For verbs, give the *infinitive* form.

1. to address ______________________
2. to adore ______________________
3. to ask ______________________
4. to attack ______________________
5. to beg, pray ______________________
6. to call ______________________
7. to carry ______________________
8. to deny ______________________
9. to disturb ______________________
10. to explore ______________________
11. to fight ______________________
12. to give ______________________
13. to guard, keep ______________________
14. to judge ______________________
15. to overcome, surpass ______________________
16. to praise ______________________
17. to prepare ______________________
18. to report ______________________
19. to sail ______________________
20. to seize ______________________
21. to set free ______________________
22. to show, point out ______________________
23. to think ______________________
24. to wait for, expect ______________________
25. always ______________________
26. never ______________________
27. not ______________________
28. now ______________________
29. often ______________________
30. then, at that time ______________________

B. Latin Sayings

1. always faithful ______________________________________
2. Fortune aids the brave. ______________________________________
3. The Mother Was Standing ______________________________________
4. Pray and work. ______________________________________
5. To err is human. ______________________________________

C. Principal Parts

1st	2nd	3rd	4th
amo			
juvo			
lavo			
sto			
sum			

D. Grammar Questions

1. The six attributes of a Latin verb are ______________________________

______________________________.

2. In English, *I praise* is the ______________ present, *I am praising* is the______________ present, and *I do praise* is the ______________ present.

3. How many words are needed to make a Latin sentence? ______________

4. The two basic parts of a sentence are the______________________________.

5. Give the three tenses that make up the present system.

____

6. The forms that provide the stems needed to conjugate a verb in all its tenses are called the

______________ ______________.

7. What is the name of the second of these forms?______________

8. The infinitive of every 1st conjugation verb ends in ______________.

9. How do you find the present stem? ______________

10. The *to be* verb shows ______________, not ______________.

11. Give the English forms of the *to be* verb. ______________

____

12. A complementary infinitive______________the action of the main verb.

13. How do you find the perfect stem?______________

14. In Latin grammar, *perfect* means______________ and *imperfect* means

______________ .

15. Name the three tenses that make up the perfect system.

____

E. Tenses

Using *to call*, give in English the 1st person singular of each tense. The first one is done for you.

1. present I call (am calling, do call)
2. imperfect______________
3. future______________
4. perfect ______________
5. pluperfect ______________
6. future perfect ______________

F. Conjugate the Latin verb **do** in all six tenses.

principal parts ______________________________

present stem: ____________________ perfect stem: ____________________

P	Present	
1		
2		
3		
	Imperfect	
1		
2		
3		
	Future	
1		
2		
3		

Perfect	
Pluperfect	
Future Perfect	

G. Conjugate the Latin verb **sum** in the present, imperfect, and future.

P	Present	
1		
2		
3		
	Imperfect	
1		
2		
3		
	Future	
1		
2		
3		

H. Form Drills

Circle tense endings (#1-3) or box any helping verbs (#4-6), parse, then translate.

Prompts Key: ***P*** = Person, ***N*** = Number, ***T*** = Tense, ***Tr*** = Translation

1. volabat *P:* ________ *N:* ________ *T:* ________ *Tr:* ________	**4.** they were telling *P:* ________ *N:* ________ *T:* ________ *Tr:* ________
2. rogatis *P:* ________ *N:* ________ *T:* ________ *Tr:* ________	**5.** I have accused *P:* ________ *N:* ________ *T:* ________ *Tr:* ________
3. stéteras *P:* ________ *N:* ________ *T:* ________ *Tr:* ________	**6.** he will have overcome *P:* ________ *N:* ________ *T:* ________ *Tr:* ________

I. Translation: Parse and label, then translate.

1. Hódie — *Tr:* ________

natabunt. — *P:* ____ *N:* ____ *T:* ________ — *Tr:* ________

Final Tr: ________

J. Bonus: Parse and label, then translate.

1. Nunc — *Tr:* ________

juvare — *Tr:* ________

sperat. — *P:* ____ *N:* ____ *T:* ________ — *Tr:* ________

Final Tr: ________

Lesson 14 Quiz

Name ______________________ Date __________

A. Vocabulary & Latin Saying: Give *dictionary form*.

1. earth, land ______________________
2. farmer ______________________
3. girl ______________________
4. Italy ______________________
5. Mary ______________________
6. poet ______________________
7. queen ______________________
8. Rome ______________________
9. sailor ______________________
10. table ______________________

Derivative: A high tableland is a ______________________.

Latin Saying: Eternal Rome ______________________

B. Grammar Questions

1. The four attributes of nouns are ______________________.
2. Nouns that name male or female persons have ______________ gender.
3. If the genitive singular of a noun ends in __________, the noun is 1st declension.

C. Decline the noun terra. Also give the case names and 1st declension case endings.

CASE	NOUN		CASE ENDINGS	
	Singular	Plural	Singular	Plural

D. Form Drills: Parse, then translate in the nominative case.

1. poetae	**2.** queens
Declension: ________ *Gender:* ________	*Declension:* ________ *Gender:* ________
Number: ________ *Case:* nominative	*Number:* ________ *Case:* nominative
Translation: ______________	*Translation:* ______________

F. Translation: Parse and label, then translate.

PROMPTS KEY: ***P*** = Person, ***N*** = Number, ***T*** = Tense, ***Tr*** = Translation

1. **Semper** | **laudamus.**

*Tr:*____________________ | *P:*____*N:*____*T:*__________

*Tr:*____________________

Final Tr:______________________________

G. Bonus: Translate. Use the space below to parse if necessary.

1. he did blame ____________________
2. I was calling ____________________

Lesson 15 Quiz

Name ________________________ Date ____________

A. Vocabulary & Latin Saying: Give *dictionary form.*

1. Christ ____________________
2. friend ____________________
3. god ____________________
4. horse ____________________
5. lamb ____________________
6. lord, master ____________________
7. slave, servant ____________________
8. son ____________________
9. world, mankind ____________________
10. year ____________________

Derivative: An ____________________ event occurs every year.

Latin Saying: In the Year of Our Lord ____________________

B. Grammar Questions

1. 2nd declension **-us** nouns are usually ____________________ in gender.
2. The subject of a verb is in the ____________________ case.

C. Decline the noun amicus. Also give the case names and 2nd declension case endings.

Case	Noun		Case Endings	

D. Form Drills: Parse, then translate in the nominative case.

1. amici

Declension: __________ *Gender:* __________

Number: __________ *Case:* nominative

Translation: ____________________

2. years

Declension: __________ *Gender:* __________

Number: __________ *Case:* nominative

Translation: ____________________

E. Translation: Parse and label, then translate.

Prompts Key: ***P*** = Person, ***N*** = Number, ***T*** = Tense, ***Tr*** = Translation

1. Optabant **orare.**

*P:*____ *N:*____ *T:*__________

*Tr:*____________________

*Tr:*____________________

Final Tr:____________________

F. Bonus: Derivative.

1. Something that is commonplace or ordinary is ____________________.

Lesson 16 Quiz

Name ______________________ Date __________

A. Vocabulary & Latin Saying: Give *dictionary form.*

1. debt, sin ______________________
2. forum, marketplace ______________________
3. gift ______________________
4. kingdom ______________________
5. rock ______________________
6. sky, heaven ______________________
7. temple ______________________
8. town ______________________
9. war ______________________
10. word ______________________

Derivative: A ______________________ agreement is one that is spoken, not written.

Latin Saying: before the war ______________________

B. Grammar Questions

1. If the genitive singular of a noun ends in __________, the noun is 2nd declension.
2. All neuter nouns obey the *neuter rule*:

   The nominative and accusative case forms are ______________________ .

   The nominative and accusative plural case ending is ______________________ .

C. Decline the noun verbum. Also give the case names and 2nd declension neuter case endings.

Case	Noun		Case Endings	

D. Form Drills: Parse, then translate in the nominative case.

Prompts Key: ***D*** = Declension, ***G*** = Gender, ***N*** = Number, ***C*** = Case, ***Tr*** = Translation

1. óppidum	**1.** gifts
D: ______ *G:* ______ *N:* ______	*D:* ______ *G:* ______ *N:* ______
C: nom. *Tr:* ______________	*C:* nom. *Tr:* ______________

E. Translation: Parse and label, then translate.

PROMPTS KEY: ***P*** = Person, ***N*** = Number, ***T*** = Tense, ***Tr*** = Translation

1. Non	**creáveris.**
*Tr:*________________	*P:*____*N:*____*T:*____________
	*Tr:*____________________________

Final Tr:____

F. Bonus: Translate. Use the space below to parse if necessary.

1. they will wait for ____________________
2. he was living in ____________________

Lesson 17 Review Quiz Name ______________________ Date __________

A. Vocabulary: Give *dictionary form.*

1. god ______________________
2. kingdom ______________________
3. Italy ______________________
4. lord, master ______________________
5. Rome ______________________
6. sailor ______________________
7. sky, heaven ______________________
8. slave, servant ______________________
9. town ______________________
10. world, mankind ______________________

B. Grammar Questions

1. The declension a noun belongs to is determined by the ______________________ ending.
2. The subject of a verb is in the ______________________ case.
3. A verb agrees with its subject in ______________ and ______________ .

C. Decline the following nouns. Also give the case names and case endings.

Case	1st Declension Noun		1st Decl. Case Endings	
	regina			

2nd Declension Masculine Noun		2nd Decl. M. Case Endings	
annus			

2nd Declension Neuter Noun		2nd Decl. N. Case Endings	
templum			

D. Translation: Parse and label, then translate.

PROMPTS KEY: *C* = Case, ***D*** = Declension, ***G*** = Gender, ***N*** = Number, ***P*** = Person, ***T*** = Tense, ***Tr*** = Translation

1. Equi | **ambulant.**

*D:*____*G:*____*N:*____*C:*________ | *P:*____*N:*____*T:*____________

*Tr:*________________________ | *Tr:*________________________

Final Tr:____

2. Agrícola | **dabat.**

*D:*____*G:*____*N:*____*C:*________ | *P:*____*N:*____*T:*____________

*Tr:*________________________ | *Tr:*________________________

Final Tr:____

E. Bonus: Latin Sayings

1. Anno Dómini (A.D.) ________________________________
2. ante bellum ________________________________
3. Roma Aeterna ________________________________

Lesson 18 Quiz Name________________________________ Date______________

A. Vocabulary & Latin Saying: Give *dictionary form*.

1. bad ______________________________
2. eternal, everlasting ______________________________
3. good ______________________________
4. great, large ______________________________
5. high, deep ______________________________
6. much (pl., many) ______________________________
7. new ______________________________
8. sacred, holy ______________________________
9. small ______________________________
10. wide, broad ______________________________

Derivative: ______________________________ is the number of degrees north or south of the equator.

Latin Saying: The Mother of Italy, Rome ______________________________

B. Grammar Question

1. In Latin, an adjective must agree with its noun in ____________________, ____________________, and ____________________, but not ______________________________ .

C. Decline the adjective **malus**.

SINGULAR			PLURAL		
m.	**f.**	**n.**	**m.**	**f.**	**n.**

D. Form Drills: Parse, then translate in the nominative case.

Prompts Key: ***D*** = Declension, ***G*** = Gender, ***N*** = Number, ***C*** = Case, ***Tr*** = Translation

1. multa débita

N. *D:* ________ *G:* ______ *N:* ______ *C:* nom.

A. *D:* ________ *G:* ______ *N:* ______ *C:* nom.

Tr: ______________________________

2. Translate **year**.

D: ________ *G:* __________ *N:* __________

C: nom. *Tr:* ______________________________

Now translate **good year**.

____

E. Translation: Parse and label, then translate.

PROMPTS KEY: ***C*** = Case, ***D*** = Declension, ***G*** = Gender, ***N*** = Number, ***P*** = Person, ***T*** = Tense, ***Tr*** = Translation

1. **Puella**	**nova**	**spectavit.**
*D:*_____ *G:*_______	*D:*_____ *G:*_______	*P:*____ *N:*____ *T:*_____________
*N:*_____ *C:*_______	*N:*_____ *C:*_______	*Tr:*______________________________
*Tr:*__________________	*Tr:*__________________	

Final Tr:____

F. Bonus

1. Adjectives of quantity or size usually ______________________________ the noun.
2. Adjectives of quality usually ________________________________the noun.

Lesson 19 Quiz

Name ____________________ Date __________

A. Vocabulary & Latin Saying: Give *dictionary form.*

1. one ____________________
2. two ____________________
3. three ____________________
4. four ____________________
5. five ____________________
6. six ____________________
7. seven ____________________
8. eight ____________________
9. nine ____________________
10. ten ____________________
11. first ____________________
12. second ____________________
13. third ____________________
14. fourth ____________________
15. fifth ____________________
16. sixth ____________________
17. seventh ____________________
18. eighth ____________________
19. ninth ____________________
20. tenth ____________________

Latin Saying: the four seasons of the year ____________________

B. Grammar Questions

1. Counting numbers are called ____________ numbers.
2. Numbers which indicate the order of things in a series are called ____________ numbers.
3. The two basic parts of a sentence are the ____________________.
4. A *predicate adjective* is an adjective that follows a ____________________, describes the ____________, and is in the ____________ case.
5. A *predicate nominative* is a noun that follows a ____________________, renames the ____________, and is in the ____________ case.

C. Decline the adjective **tértius**.

SINGULAR			PLURAL		
m.	**f.**	**n.**	**m.**	**f.**	**n.**

D. Translation: Parse and label, then translate.

PROMPTS KEY: ***C*** = Case, ***D*** = Declension, ***G*** = Gender, ***N*** = Number, ***P*** = Person, ***T*** = Tense, ***Tr*** = Translation

1. **Caelum**	**est**	**aeternum.**
*D:*____ *G:*____ *N:*____ *C:*______	*P:*____ *N:*____ *T:*______________	*D:*____ *G:*____ *N:*____ *C:*_____
*Tr:*______________________	*Tr:*______________________________	*Tr:*____________________

Final Tr:____

E. Bonus: Parse and label, then translate.

1. **Prima**	**verba**	**non**	**perturbaverunt.**
*D:*_____ *G:*_______	*D:*_____ *G:*_______	*Tr:*_____________	*P:*____ *N:*____ *T:*______________
*N:*_____ *C:*_______	*N:*_____ *C:*_______		*Tr:*____________________________
*Tr:*_____________	*Tr:*_____________		________________________________

Final Tr:____

Lesson 20 Test: Unit III

Name ______________________ Date __________

A. Vocabulary: Give *dictionary form.*

1. bad ______________________
2. Christ ______________________
3. earth, land ______________________
4. first ______________________
5. five ______________________
6. friend ______________________
7. god ______________________
8. good ______________________
9. great, large ______________________
10. high, deep ______________________
11. horse ______________________
12. kingdom ______________________
13. Mary ______________________
14. much (pl., many) ______________________
15. new ______________________
16. one ______________________
17. queen ______________________
18. sacred, holy ______________________
19. sailor ______________________
20. sky, heaven ______________________
21. slave, servant ______________________
22. son ______________________
23. table ______________________
24. ten ______________________
25. third ______________________
26. town ______________________
27. war ______________________
28. wide, broad ______________________
29. world, mankind ______________________
30. year ______________________

B. Latin Sayings

1. before the war ______________________
2. Eternal Rome ______________________
3. the four seasons of the year ______________________
4. In the Year of Our Lord ______________________
5. The Mother of Italy, Rome ______________________

C. Grammar Questions

1. The four attributes of nouns are ______________________

   ______________________.
2. Nouns that name male or female persons have ______________________ gender.
3. Nouns that name non-living things have ______________________ gender.
4. Latin does not have the English articles __________, __________, and __________.
5. The subject of a verb is in the ______________________ case.
6. All neuter nouns obey the *neuter rule*:

   The nominative and accusative case forms are ______________________ .

   The nominative and accusative plural case ending is ______________________ .

C. Grammar Questions, continued

7. The declension a noun belongs to is determined by the ______________________ ending.
8. The subject and verb must agree in ______________ and ______________ .
9. In Latin, an adjective must agree with its noun in ______________, ______________, and ______________, but not ______________________ .
10. Counting numbers are called ______________ numbers.
11. Numbers which indicate the order of things in a series are called ______________ numbers.
12. The two basic parts of a sentence are the ______________________________.
13. A ______________________________ follows a linking verb and renames the subject.
14. A ______________________________ follows a linking verb and describes the subject.
15. What is the subject case? ______________ The direct object case? ______________

    The indirect object case? ______________ The possessive case? ______________

    The *in/by/with/from* case? ______________ The *to/for* case? ______________

    The *of* case? ______________

D. Decline the adjective **parvus**.

SINGULAR			PLURAL		
m.	f.	n.	m.	f.	n.

E. Form Drills: Parse, then translate in the nominative case.

Prompts Key: ***D*** = Declension, ***G*** = Gender, ***N*** = Number, ***C*** = Case, ***Tr*** = Translation

1. quartus agnus	**2.** Translate **kingdoms**.
N. *D:* ______ *G:* ______ *N:* ______ *C:* nom.	*D:* ______ *G:* ______ *N:* ______
A. *D:* ______ *G:* ______ *N:* ______ *C:* nom.	*C:* nom. *Tr:* ______________
Tr: ______________________	Now translate **large kingdoms**.
	______________________

F. Translation: Parse and label, then translate.

PROMPTS KEY: *C* = Case, ***D*** = Declension, ***G*** = Gender, ***N*** = Number, ***P*** = Person, ***T*** = Tense, ***Tr*** = Translation

1. Amicus
*D:*____ *G:*____ *N:*____ *C:*________
*Tr:*______________________

erit
*P:*____ *N:*____ *T:*________________
*Tr:*______________________

poeta.
*D:*____ *G:*____ *N:*____ *C:*________
*Tr:*______________________

Final Tr:____

2. Itália
*D:*______ *G:*________
*N:*______ *C:*________
*Tr:*______________

numquam
*Tr:*______________

fuit
*P:*_____ *N:*_____ *T:*______________
*Tr:*______________________

parva.
*D:*______ *G:*________
*N:*______ *C:*________
*Tr:*______________

Final Tr:____

G. Bonus

The answers will be derivatives of the following Latin words.

equus	novus	regnum	terra

1. The ______________________ was a new form of literature in the seventeenth century.
2. The ______________________ of Augustus was peaceful.
3. The study of horses is called ______________________ science.
4. American settlers moving west had to go through Native American ______________________.

Lesson 21 Quiz

Name______________________________ Date____________

A. Vocabulary & Latin Saying: Give the *full* dictionary form.

1. brother ______________________
2. father ______________________
3. king ______________________
4. leader ______________________
5. mother ______________________
6. sister ______________________
7. soldier ______________________

Derivative: In a hospital, the location where babies are born is called the ______________________ ward.

Latin Saying: nurturing mother ______________________

B. Grammar Questions

1. All nouns whose genitive singular ends in ____________ belong to the 3rd declension.
2. How do you find the stem of <u>any</u> Latin noun? ______________________

____

C. Decline the noun **frater**. Also give the 3rd declension *masculine/feminine* case endings.

NOUN		CASE ENDINGS	

D. Form Drills: Parse, then translate in the nominative case.

Prompts Key: ***D*** = Declension, ***G*** = Gender, ***N*** = Number, ***C*** = Case, ***Tr*** = Translation

1. Rex Sanctus

N. *D:* _______ *G:* _____ *N:* ______ *C:* nom.

A. *D:* _______ *G:* _____ *N:* ______ *C:* nom.

Tr: ______________________

2. Translate **soldiers**.

D: ________ *G:* _________ *N:* ___________

C: nom. *Tr:* ______________________

Now translate **good soldiers**.

____

E. Translation: Parse and label, then translate.

PROMPTS KEY: ***C*** = Case, ***D*** = Declension, ***G*** = Gender, ***N*** = Number, ***P*** = Person, ***T*** = Tense, ***Tr*** = Translation

1. **Mater** | **semper** | **laborat.**

*D:*____*G:*____*N:*____*C:*________
*Tr:*____________________
*Tr:*____________________
*P:*____*N:*____*T:*____________
*Tr:*____________________

Final Tr:______________________________________

2. **Duces** | **mali** | **vulneráverint.**

*D:*____*G:*____*N:*____*C:*______
*Tr:*____________________
*D:*____*G:*____*N:*____*C:*______
*Tr:*____________________
*P:*____*N:*____*T:*____________
*Tr:*____________________
____

Final Tr:______________________________________

F. Bonus: Give a synopsis of **aro** in the *2nd person singular.*

2nd Sing. present ____________________
2nd Sing. imperfect ____________________
2nd Sing. future ____________________
2nd Sing. perfect____________________
2nd Sing. pluperfect____________________
2nd Sing. future perfect____________________

Lesson 22 Quiz

Name ______________________________ Date ____________

A. Vocabulary & Latin Saying: Give the *full* dictionary form.

1. bread ____________________
2. cross ____________________
3. custom ____________________
4. dog ____________________
5. foot ____________________
6. law ____________________
7. light ____________________
8. peace ____________________
9. sun ____________________
10. voice ____________________

Derivative: A handle is to the hand what a ____________________ is to the foot.

Latin Saying: The Roman Peace ____________________

B. Grammar Questions

1. How can you know the gender of a 3rd declension noun? ____________________

____

2. How do you find the stem of a Latin noun? ____________________

____

C. Decline the noun **canis**. Also give the 3rd declension *masculine/feminine* case endings.

NOUN		CASE ENDINGS	

D. Form Drills: Parse, then translate in the nominative case.

Prompts Key: ***D*** = Declension, ***G*** = Gender, ***N*** = Number, ***C*** = Case, ***Tr*** = Translation

1. leges novae

N. *D:* ______ *G:* ______ *N:* ______ *C:* nom.

A. *D:* ______ *G:* ______ *N:* ______ *C:* nom.

Tr: ____________________

2. Translate **feet.**

D: ______ *G:* ______ *N:* ______

C: nom. *Tr:* ____________________

Now translate **wide feet.**

____

E. Translation: Parse and label, then translate.

PROMPTS KEY: ***C*** = Case, ***D*** = Declension, ***G*** = Gender, ***N*** = Number, ***P*** = Person, ***T*** = Tense, ***Tr*** = Translation

1. **Quáttuor**	**canes**	**demonstrabant.**
*D:*____ *G:*____ *N:*____ *C:*________	*D:*____ *G:*____ *N:*____ *C:*________	*P:*____ *N:*____ *T:*________
*Tr:*________________	*Tr:*________________	*Tr:*________________

Final Tr:________________________________

2. **Sol**	**nunc**	**errat!**
*D:*____ *G:*____ *N:*____ *C:*________	*Tr:*________________	*P:*____ *N:*____ *T:*________
*Tr:*________________		*Tr:*________________

Final Tr:________________________________

F. Bonus: Parse and label, then translate.

1. **Panis**	**erit**	**donum**	**magnum.**
*D:*________	*P:*____ *N:*____ *T:*________	*D:*________	*D:*________
*G:*________	*Tr:*________________	*G:*________	*G:*________
*N:*________		*N:*________	*N:*________
*C:*________		*C:*________	*C:*________
*Tr:*________		*Tr:*________	*Tr:*________

Final Tr:________________________________

Lesson 23 Quiz

Name________________________________ Date____________

A. Vocabulary & Latin Saying: Give the *full* dictionary form.

1. head ________________________________
2. heart ________________________________
3. lamp ________________________________
4. name ________________________________
5. river ________________________________

Derivative: I want to ________________________ Carla to be captain of the volleyball team.

Latin Saying: Head of the World ____

B. Grammar Questions

1. All nouns whose genitive singular ends in ____________ belong to the 3rd declension.
2. All neuter nouns obey the *neuter rule*:

   The nominative and accusative case forms are ________________________ .

   The nominative and accusative plural case ending is ____________________ .

C. Decline the noun **caput**. Also give the 3rd declension *neuter* case endings.

NOUN		CASE ENDINGS	

D. Form Drills: Parse, then translate in the nominative case.

PROMPTS KEY: ***D*** = Declension, ***G*** = Gender, ***N*** = Number, ***C*** = Case, ***Tr*** = Translation

1. alta flúmina	**2.** Translate **heart**.
N. *D:* _______ *G:* _____ *N:* ______ *C:* nom.	*D:* ________ *G:* _________ *N:* ___________
A. *D:* _______ *G:* _____ *N:* ______ *C:* nom.	*C:* nom. *Tr:* ______________________
Tr: ________________________________	Now translate **much heart**.
	________________________________

E. Translation: Parse and label, then translate.

Prompts Key: ***C*** = Case, ***D*** = Declension, ***G*** = Gender, ***N*** = Number, ***P*** = Person, ***T*** = Tense, ***Tr*** = Translation

1. **Fratres** — *D:*____ *G:*____ *N:*____ *C:*________ *Tr:*________________________
   narrare — *Tr:*________________
   parabant. — *P:*____ *N:*____ *T:*________________ *Tr:*________________________

   Final Tr:____

2. **Primum** — *D:*______ *G:*________ *N:*______ *C:*________ *Tr:*______________
   nomen — *D:*______ *G:*________ *N:*______ *C:*________ *Tr:*______________
   numquam — *Tr:*________________
   mutat. — *P:*_____ *N:*_____ *T:*________________ *Tr:*________________________

   Final Tr:____

F. Bonus: Give a synopsis of **creo** in the *3rd person plural*.

3rd Pl. present ______________________________ 3rd Pl. perfect ______________________________

3rd Pl. imperfect ______________________________ 3rd Pl. pluperfect ______________________________

3rd Pl. future ______________________________ 3rd Pl. future perfect ______________________________

Lesson 24 Review Quiz Name ______________ Date ________

A. Vocabulary: Give the *full* dictionary form.

1. bread ______________
2. brother ______________
3. cross ______________
4. custom ______________
5. dog ______________
6. father ______________
7. foot ______________
8. head ______________
9. heart ______________
10. king ______________
11. lamp ______________
12. law ______________
13. leader ______________
14. light ______________
15. mother ______________
16. name ______________
17. peace ______________
18. river ______________
19. sister ______________
20. soldier ______________
21. sun ______________
22. voice ______________

Latin Saying: King of Kings ______________

B. Grammar Questions

1. How can you know the gender of a 3rd declension noun? ______________
2. The subject of a verb is in the ______________ case and the direct object of a verb is in the ______________ case.

C. Decline the following 3rd declension nouns. Also give the case names and case endings.

Case	3rd Declension Neuter Noun		3rd Decl. N. Case Endings	
	flumen			

3rd Decl. Masculine/Feminine Noun		3rd Decl. Masculine/Feminine Noun		3rd Decl. M/F Case Endings	
pax		miles			

D. Form Drills: Parse, then translate in the nominative case.

Prompts Key: ***D*** = Declension, ***G*** = Gender, ***N*** = Number, ***C*** = Case, ***Tr*** = Translation

1. nomen sanctum	**2.** Translate **voices.**
N. *D:* _______ *G:* _____ *N:* _____ *C:* nom.	*D:* ________ *G:* _________ *N:* ___________
A. *D:* _______ *G:* _____ *N:* _____ *C:* nom.	*C:* nom. *Tr:* ___________________________
Tr: ____	Now translate **good voices.**
	____

E. Translation: Parse and label, then translate.

Prompts Key: ***C*** = Case, ***D*** = Declension, ***G*** = Gender, ***N*** = Number, ***P*** = Person, ***T*** = Tense, ***Tr*** = Translation

1. Multa	**regna**	**Romam**	**oppugnáverant.**
*D:*_____*G:*_______	*D:*_____*G:*_______	*D:*_____*G:*_______	*P:*_____*N:*_____*T:*_____________
*N:*_____*C:*_______	*N:*_____*C:*_______	*N:*_____*C:*_______	*Tr:*___________________________
*Tr:*______________	*Tr:*______________	*Tr:*______________	______________________________

Final Tr:____

2. Pater	**tres**	**puellas**	**juvabit.**
*D:*_____*G:*_______	*D:*_____*G:*_______	*D:*_____*G:*_______	*P:*_____*N:*_____*T:*_____________
*N:*_____*C:*_______	*N:*_____*C:*_______	*N:*_____*C:*_______	*Tr:*___________________________
*Tr:*______________	*Tr:*______________	*Tr:*______________	

Final Tr:____

F. Bonus: Latin Sayings

1. alma mater ____
2. Head of the World ____
3. The Roman Peace____

Lesson 25 Quiz

Name________________________________ Date______________

A. Vocabulary & Latin Saying: Give *dictionary form*.

1. army________________________________
2. arrival ________________________________
3. fear ________________________________
4. fruit ________________________________
5. hand________________________________
6. harbor ________________________________
7. house, home ________________________________
8. lake________________________________
9. senate________________________________
10. spirit________________________________

Derivative: ________________________________labor is work done by hand.

Latin Saying: The Senate and People of Rome

____

B. Grammar Questions

1. The genitive singular of a 4th declension noun always ends in__________.
2. Most 4th declension nouns are ________________________in gender.

C. Decline the noun **manus**. Also give the 4th declension case endings.

NOUN		CASE ENDINGS	

D. Form Drills: Parse, then translate in the nominative case.

Prompts Key: ***D*** = Declension, ***G*** = Gender, ***N*** = Number, ***C*** = Case, ***Tr*** = Translation

1. Translate **fruits.**	**2.** Translate **senate.**
D: ________ *G:* ________ *N:* __________	*D:* ________ *G:* ________ *N:* __________
C: nom. *Tr:* ____________________	*C:* nom. *Tr:* ____________________
Now translate **large fruits.**	Now translate **small senate.**
______________________________	______________________________

E. Translation: Parse and label, then translate.

PROMPTS KEY: ***C*** = Case, ***D*** = Declension, ***G*** = Gender, ***N*** = Number, ***P*** = Person, ***T*** = Tense, ***Tr*** = Translation

1. **Fílius** *D:*____*G:*____*N:*____*C:*________ *Tr:*____________________

   adventum *D:*____*G:*____*N:*____*C:*________ *Tr:*____________________

   nuntiáverat. *P:*_____*N:*_____*T:*________________ *Tr:*____________________

   Final Tr:____

2. **Mílites** *D:*______*G:*________ *N:*______*C:*________ *Tr:*________________

   latum *D:*______*G:*________ *N:*______*C:*________ *Tr:*________________

   lacum *D:*______*G:*________ *N:*______*C:*________ *Tr:*________________

   nataverunt. *P:*_____*N:*_____*T:*________________ *Tr:*____________________ ____________________

   Final Tr:____

F. Bonus: Irregular Principal Parts. Complete the chart.

1st	2nd	3rd	4th
do			
juvo			
lavo			
sto			

Lesson 26 Quiz

Name ______________________________ Date ____________

A. Vocabulary & Latin Saying: Give the *full* dictionary form.

1. day ______________________________
2. face ______________________________
3. faith, trust ______________________________
4. hope ______________________________
5. thing, matter, affair, business ______________________________

Derivative: A record of one's daily activity is called a ______________________ .

Latin Saying: Seize the day. ____

B. Grammar Questions

1. The genitive singular of a 5th declension noun always ends in __________.
2. Circle the correct choice. Genitive singular forms in the 5th declension can have up to 1 2 3 consecutive vowels. Are they all pronounced? ______________

C. Decline the noun dies. Also give the 5th declension case endings.

NOUN		CASE ENDINGS	

D. Form Drills: Parse, then translate in the nominative case.

Prompts Key: ***D*** = Declension, ***G*** = Gender, ***N*** = Number, ***C*** = Case, ***Tr*** = Translation

1. Translate **faith**.	2. Translate **things**.
D: ________ *G:* ________ *N:* ________	*D:* ________ *G:* ________ *N:* ________
C: nom. *Tr:* ____________________	*C:* nom. *Tr:* ____________________
Now translate **eternal faith**.	Now translate **good things**.
______________________________	______________________________

E. Translation: Parse and label, then translate.

PROMPTS KEY: *C* = Case, ***D*** = Declension, ***G*** = Gender, ***N*** = Number, ***P*** = Person, ***T*** = Tense, ***Tr*** = Translation

1. **Canis** *D:*____ *G:*_____ *N:*____ *C:*________ *Tr:*____________________
   fácies *D:*____ *G:*_____ *N:*____ *C:*________ *Tr:*____________________
   spectabat. *P:*_____ *N:*_____ *T:*______________ *Tr:*____________________ ____________________

   Final Tr:____

2. **Terram** *D:*______ *G:*________ *N:*______ *C:*________ *Tr:*______________
   Sanctam *D:*______ *G:*________ *N:*______ *C:*________ *Tr:*______________
   exércitus *D:*______ *G:*________ *N:*______ *C:*________ *Tr:*______________
   exploravit. *P:*_____ *N:*_____ *T:*______________ *Tr:*____________________ ____________________

   Final Tr:____

F. Bonus: Parse and label, then translate.

1. **Soror** *D:*______ *G:*________ *N:*______ *C:*________ *Tr:*______________
   saepe *Tr:*______________
   volare *Tr:*______________
   amat. *P:*_____ *N:*_____ *T:*______________ *Tr:*____________________

   Final Tr:____

Lesson 27 Test: Unit IV

Name________________________________ Date_____________

A. Vocabulary

Give *dictionary form*. Remember to include the full genitive singular for 3rd & 5th declension nouns.

1. army ______________________
2. arrival ______________________
3. bread ______________________
4. brother ______________________
5. cross ______________________
6. custom ______________________
7. day ______________________
8. dog ______________________
9. face ______________________
10. faith, trust ______________________
11. father ______________________
12. fear ______________________
13. foot ______________________
14. fruit ______________________
15. hand ______________________
16. harbor ______________________
17. head ______________________
18. heart ______________________
19. hope ______________________
20. house, home ______________________
21. king ______________________
22. lake ______________________
23. lamp ______________________
24. law ______________________
25. leader ______________________
26. light ______________________
27. mother ______________________
28. name ______________________
29. peace ______________________
30. river ______________________
31. senate ______________________
32. sister ______________________
33. soldier ______________________
34. spirit ______________________
35. sun ______________________
36. thing, matter, affair, business ______________________
37. voice ______________________

B. Latin Sayings

1. The Senate and People of Rome ______________________
2. nurturing mother ______________________
3. The Roman Peace ______________________
4. King of Kings ______________________
5. Seize the day. ______________________
6. Head of the World ______________________

C. Grammar Questions

1. The declension a noun belongs to is determined by the ________________ ending.
2. How do you find the stem of a Latin noun? ________________

   ____
3. How can you know the gender of a 3rd declension noun? ________________

   ____
4. The subject of a verb is in the ________________ case and the direct object of a verb is in the ________________ case.
5. 1st/2nd declension adjectives can modify nouns of the ________________ declensions.
6. In Latin, an adjective must agree with its noun in ________________, ________________, and ________________, but not ________________ .

D. Decline the following nouns. Also give the case names.

Case	Singular	Plural
	rex	

Singular	Plural
cor	

Singular	Plural
metus	

Singular	Plural
fides	

E. Form Drills: Parse, then translate in the nominative (#1, 3) or accusative (#2, 4) case.

PROMPTS KEY: *D* = Declension, ***G*** = Gender, ***N*** = Number, ***C*** = Case, ***Tr*** = Translation

1. lex mala **N.** *D:* _______ *G:* _____ *N:* ______ *C:* nom. **A.** *D:* _______ *G:* _____ *N:* ______ *C:* nom. *Tr:* ________________________________	**3.** Translate **head**. *D:* ________ *G:* _________ *N:* ___________ *C:* nom. *Tr:* _________________________ Now translate **wide head**. ________________________________
2. decem fácies **N.** *D:* _______ *G:* _____ *N:* ______ *C:* acc. **A.** *D:* _______ *G:* _____ *N:* ______ *C:* acc. *Tr:* ________________________________	**4.** Translate **hands**. *D:* ________ *G:* _________ *N:* ___________ *C:* acc. *Tr:* _________________________ Now translate **small hands**. ________________________________

F. Translation: Parse and label, then translate.

PROMPTS KEY: *C* = Case, ***D*** = Declension, ***G*** = Gender, ***N*** = Number, ***P*** = Person, ***T*** = Tense, ***Tr*** = Translation

1. Panis	**bonus**	**fratres**	**temptabat.**
*D:*_____*G:*_______	*D:*_____*G:*_______	*D:*_____*G:*_______	*P:*____*N:*____*T:*_________
*N:*_____*C:*_______	*N:*_____*C:*_______	*N:*_____*C:*_______	*Tr:*____________________
*Tr:*_______________	*Tr:*_______________	*Tr:*_______________	____________________

Final Tr:____

2. Tértium	**diem**	**nunc**	**exspectábimus.**
*D:*_____*G:*_______	*D:*_____*G:*_______	*Tr:*___________	*P:*____*N:*____*T:*_________
*N:*_____*C:*_______	*N:*_____*C:*_______		*Tr:*____________________
*Tr:*_______________	*Tr:*_______________		

Final Tr:____

G. Bonus: The answers will be derivatives of the following Latin words.

adventus	cor	fides	pater	sol

1. An eclipse of the sun is a ______________________________eclipse.
2. Another word for faithfulness is______________________________.
3. The season of ______________________________ is the four weeks before Christmas.
4. The noble people of Rome were called______________________________ .
5. Even though they did not know us, they gave us a ___________________________ welcome.

Lesson 28 Test: Units III & IV

Name ______________________________ Date ____________

A. Vocabulary: Give *dictionary form.*

1. army ______________________
2. bad ______________________
3. brother ______________________
4. Christ ______________________
5. day ______________________
6. earth, land ______________________
7. faith, trust ______________________
8. father ______________________
9. fear ______________________
10. first ______________________
11. foot ______________________
12. friend ______________________
13. god ______________________
14. good ______________________
15. great, large ______________________
16. hand ______________________
17. harbor ______________________
18. head ______________________
19. hope ______________________
20. Italy ______________________
21. king ______________________
22. kingdom ______________________
23. law ______________________
24. leader ______________________
25. light ______________________
26. lord, master ______________________
27. Mary ______________________
28. mother ______________________
29. much, many ______________________
30. name ______________________
31. new ______________________
32. peace ______________________
33. river ______________________
34. Rome ______________________
35. sacred, holy ______________________
36. sailor ______________________
37. senate ______________________
38. sky, heaven ______________________
39. slave, servant ______________________
40. small ______________________
41. soldier ______________________
42. son ______________________
43. spirit ______________________
44. third ______________________
45. town ______________________
46. voice ______________________
47. war ______________________
48. wide, broad ______________________
49. world, mankind ______________________
50. year ______________________

B. Latin Sayings

1. before the war ______________________
2. Eternal Rome ______________________
3. In the Year of Our Lord ______________________
4. nurturing mother ______________________
5. The Roman Peace ______________________
6. Seize the day. ______________________

C. Grammar Questions

1. The four attributes of nouns are ____

____.

2. Latin does not have the English articles__________, ____________, and___________.

3. All neuter nouns obey the *neuter rule*:

   The nominative and accusative case forms are_______________________ .

   The nominative and accusative plural case ending is __________________ .

4. The declension a noun belongs to is determined by the ______________________ending.

5. The subject and verb must agree in ___________________ and ____________________ .

6. In Latin, an adjective must agree with its noun in_________________,___________________,

   and __________________, but not_____________________________ .

7. Counting numbers are called ____________________ numbers.

8. Numbers which indicate the order of things in a series are called _________________numbers.

9. The two basic parts of a sentence are the_____________________________________.

10. A_______________________________________follows a linking verb and **renames** the subject.

11. A________________________________ follows a linking verb and **describes** the subject.

12. What is the subject case? ____________________the direct object case? _______________

    the indirect object case? _____________________the possessive case?_________________

    the *in/by/with/from* case? ___________________the *to/for* case?______________________

    the *of* case? ________________________

13. How do you find the stem of a Latin noun? ____

    ____

14. The subject is in the___________________________________case and the direct object is in

    the ________________________________ case.

D. Decline the following nouns. Also give the case names.

Case	Singular	Plural
	res	

Singular	Plural
fructus	

Singular	Plural
equus	

Singular	Plural
sol	

Singular	Plural
flumen	

Singular	Plural
regnum	

Singular	Plural
puella	

E. Form Drills: Parse, then translate in the nominative (#1, 3) or accusative (#2, 4) case.

PROMPTS KEY: ***D*** = Declension, ***G*** = Gender, ***N*** = Number, ***C*** = Case, ***Tr*** = Translation

1. multa óppida

N. *D:* ________ *G:* ______ *N:* _______ *C:* nom.

A. *D:* ________ *G:* ______ *N:* _______ *C:* nom.

Tr: ____

3. Translate **home**.

D: _________ *G:* __________ *N:* ____________

C: nom. *Tr:* ___________________________

Now translate **eternal home**.

____

2. ducem magnum

N. *D:* ________ *G:* ______ *N:* _______ *C:* acc.

A. *D:* ________ *G:* ______ *N:* _______ *C:* acc.

Tr: ____

4. Translate **lamp**.

D: _________ *G:* __________ *N:* ____________

C: acc. *Tr:* ___________________________

Now translate **second lamp**.

____

F. Translation: Parse and label, then translate.

PROMPTS KEY: ***C*** = Case, ***D*** = Declension, ***G*** = Gender, ***N*** = Number, ***P*** = Person, ***T*** = Tense, ***Tr*** = Translation

1. Septem	**reges**	**Romam**	**serváverunt.**
*D:*________	*D:*________	*D:*________	*P:*____*N:*____*T:*________
*G:*________	*G:*________	*G:*________	*Tr:*________
*N:*________	*N:*________	*N:*________	
*C:*________	*C:*________	*C:*________	
*Tr:*________	*Tr:*________	*Tr:*________	

Final Tr:________________________

2. Mos	**mílites**	**novos**	**non**	**perturbáverit.**
*D:*________	*D:*________	*D:*________	*Tr:*________	*P:*____*N:*____*T:*________
*G:*________	*G:*________	*G:*________		*Tr:*________
*N:*________	*N:*________	*N:*________		________
*C:*________	*C:*________	*C:*________		
*Tr:*________	*Tr:*________	*Tr:*________		

Final Tr:________________________

____

G. Bonus: Parse and label, then translate.

1. Semper	**mundus**	**sperare**	**optábit.**
*Tr:*________	*D:*________	*Tr:*________	*P:*____*N:*____*T:*________
	*G:*________		*Tr:*________
	*N:*________		________
	*C:*________		
	*Tr:*________		

Final Tr:________________________

Lesson 29 Quiz Name____________________ Date__________

A. Vocabulary & Latin Saying: Give *first two principal parts*.

1. to be silent ____________________
2. to have ____________________
3. to hold ____________________
4. to move ____________________
5. to owe, ought ____________________
6. to rejoice ____________________
7. to see ____________________
8. to sit ____________________
9. to teach ____________________
10. to warn ____________________

Derivative: Janice, who is usually ____________________, could not stop running around.

Latin Saying: I see and am silent. ____________________

B. Grammar Questions

1. To find the present stem of a 2nd conjugation verb, drop __________ from the infinitive.
2. The stem vowel of the 2nd conjugation is __________.

C. Conjugate the verb **téneo** in the *present* tense with meanings.

first two principal parts: ____________________ pres. stem: __________

P	LATIN		ENGLISH MEANINGS	
	Singular	Plural	Singular	Plural
1				
2				
3				

D. Form Drills: Circle tense endings (#1-2) or box any helping verbs (#3-4), parse, then translate.

Prompts Key: ***Cj*** = Conjugation, ***P*** = Person, ***N*** = Number, ***T*** = Tense, ***Tr*** = Translation

1. docent *Cj:*____ *P:* ____ *N:*____ *T:* ________ *Tr:* ________________	**3.** we are sitting *Cj:*____ *P:* ____ *N:*____ *T:* ________ *Tr:* ________________
2. habes *Cj:*____ *P:* ____ *N:*____ *T:* ________ *Tr:* ________________	**4.** I hold *Cj:*____ *P:* ____ *N:*____ *T:* ________ *Tr:* ________________

E. Translation: Parse and label, then translate.

Key: ***C*** = Case, ***Cj*** = Conjugation, ***D*** = Declension, ***G*** = Gender, ***N*** = Number, ***P*** = Person, ***T*** = Tense, ***Tr*** = Translation

1. **Pater**	**latas**	**mensas**	**movet.**
*D:*____ *G:*____	*D:*____ *G:*____	*D:*____ *G:*____	*Cj:*____ *P:*____
*N:*____ *C:*____	*N:*____ *C:*____	*N:*____ *C:*____	*N:*____ *T:*____
*Tr:*____	*Tr:*____	*Tr:*____	*Tr:*____

Final Tr:________

2. **Spíritus**	**Sanctus**	**corda**	**mala**	**monet.**
*D:*____	*D:*____	*D:*____	*D:*____	*Cj:*____ *P:*____
*G:*____	*G:*____	*G:*____	*G:*____	*N:*____ *T:*____
*N:*____	*N:*____	*N:*____	*N:*____	*Tr:*____
*C:*____	*C:*____	*C:*____	*C:*____	
*Tr:*____	*Tr:*____	*Tr:*____	*Tr:*____	

Final Tr:________

F. Bonus: Parse and label, then translate.

1. **Narrare**	**nonus**	**nauta**	**debet.**
*Tr:*____	*D:*____	*D:*____	*Cj:*____ *P:*____
	*G:*____	*G:*____	*N:*____ *T:*____
	*N:*____	*N:*____	*Tr:*____
	*C:*____	*C:*____	
	*Tr:*____	*Tr:*____	

Final Tr:________

Lesson 30 Quiz

Name________________________________ Date_____________

A. Vocabulary & Latin Saying: Give the *first two principal parts.*

1. to appear ______________________________
2. to be strong, be well ______________________________
3. to beware of, guard against ______________________________
4. to burn, be on fire ______________________________
5. to fear, be afraid of ______________________________
6. to frighten ______________________________
7. to order, command ______________________________
8. to prevent ______________________________
9. to remain, stay ______________________________
10. to respond, answer ______________________________

Derivative: My dog is ______________________________ around cats and ferocious around other dogs.

Latin Saying: Beware of the dog. ______________________________

B. Grammar Questions

1. A ______________________________ infinitive completes the action of the main verb.
2. Compare the 1st and 2nd conjugations.

Conjugation	*Stem Vowel*	*Infinitive Ending*	*1st Person Singular Present*
1st	________	________	________
2nd	________	________	________

C. Conjugate the verb **váleo** in the present, imperfect, and future tenses.

first two principal parts: ______________________________ pres. stem: __________

P	Present		Imperfect	
1				
2				
3				

Future	

D. Form Drills

Circle tense endings (#1-2) or box any helping verbs (#3-4), parse, then translate.

PROMPTS KEY: ***Cj*** = Conjugation, ***P*** = Person, ***N*** = Number, ***T*** = Tense, ***Tr*** = Translation

1. terrebunt *Cj:* _____ *P:* ____ *N:* _____ *T:* ____________ *Tr:* ______________________________________	**3.** it will appear *Cj:* _____ *P:* ____ *N:* _____ *T:* ____________ *Tr:* ______________________________________
2. prohibebam *Cj:* _____ *P:* ____ *N:* _____ *T:* ____________ *Tr:* ______________________________________	**4.** you were responding *Cj:* _____ *P:* ____ *N:* _____ *T:* ____________ *Tr:* ______________________________________

E. Translation: Parse and label, then translate.

KEY: ***C*** = Case, ***Cj*** = Conjugation, ***D*** = Declension, ***G*** = Gender, ***N*** = Number, ***P*** = Person, ***T*** = Tense, ***Tr*** = Translation

1. **Parvi**	**agni**	**manēre**	**timent.**
D: __________	*D:* __________	*Cj:* _____	*Cj:* _____ *P:* _____
G: __________	*G:* __________	*Tr:* __________	*N:* _____ *T:* _____
N: __________	*N:* __________		*Tr:* __________
C: __________	*C:* __________		__________
Tr: __________	*Tr:* __________		

Final Tr: ____

2. **Mater**	**altum**	**solem**	**saepe**	**cavebat.**
D: __________	*D:* __________	*D:* __________	*Tr:* __________	*Cj:* _____ *P:* _____
G: __________	*G:* __________	*G:* __________		*N:* _____ *T:* _____
N: __________	*N:* __________	*N:* __________		*Tr:* __________
C: __________	*C:* __________	*C:* __________		__________
Tr: __________	*Tr:* __________	*Tr:* __________		

Final Tr: ____

____

F. Bonus: Give a synopsis of **puto** in the *3rd person singular.*

3rd Sing. present ______________________

3rd Sing. imperfect ______________________

3rd Sing. future ______________________

3rd Sing. perfect ______________________

3rd Sing. pluperfect ______________________

3rd Sing. future perfect ______________________

Lesson 31 Quiz

Name______________________________ Date____________

A. Vocabulary & Latin Saying: Give the *principal parts* of the following verbs.

1st	2nd	3rd	4th
móneo			
hábeo			
árdeo			
dóceo			
júbeo			
máneo			
téneo			
tímeo			
váleo			

Latin Saying: To teach, to delight, to move ______________________________

B. Grammar Questions

1. The forms that provide the stems needed to conjugate a verb in all its tenses are called the

    ______________________ ______________________.

2. Give the regular endings for the principal parts of 2nd conjugation verbs. ______________________

C. Form Drills

Circle tense endings (#1-2) or box any helping verbs (#3-4), parse, then translate.

PROMPTS KEY: ***Cj*** = Conjugation, ***P*** = Person, ***N*** = Number, ***T*** = Tense, ***Tr*** = Translation

1. jubebatis *Cj:*_____ *P:* _____ *N:*_____ *T:* ____________ *Tr:* ______________________________	**3.** he warns *Cj:*_____ *P:* _____ *N:*_____ *T:* ____________ *Tr:* ______________________________
2. tenebis *Cj:*_____ *P:* _____ *N:*_____ *T:* ____________ *Tr:* ______________________________	**4.** I will remain *Cj:*_____ *P:* _____ *N:*_____ *T:* ____________ *Tr:* ______________________________

D. Translation: Parse and label, then translate.

KEY: C = Case, **Cj** = Conjugation, **D** = Declension, **G** = Gender, **N** = Number, **P** = Person, **T** = Tense, **Tr** = Translation

1. **Multae** | **luces** | **tum** | **apparebant.**

Multae	luces	tum	apparebant.
*D:*______	*D:*______	*Tr:*______	*Cj:*____ *P:*____
*G:*______	*G:*______	______	*N:*____ *T:*____
*N:*______	*N:*______		*Tr:*______
*C:*______	*C:*______		______
*Tr:*______	*Tr:*______		

Final Tr:____________________

2. **Heri** | **templum** | **novum** | **ardebat.**

Heri	templum	novum	ardebat.
*Tr:*______	*D:*______	*D:*______	*Cj:*____ *P:*____
	*G:*______	*G:*______	*N:*____ *T:*____
	*N:*______	*N:*______	*Tr:*______
	*C:*______	*C:*______	______
	*Tr:*______	*Tr:*______	

Final Tr:____________________

E. Bonus: Parse and label, then translate.

1. **The bad king is ever denying Christ!**

(The) bad	king	ever	is denying	Christ!
*D:*______	*D:*______	*Tr:*______	*Cj:*____ *P:*____	*D:*______
*G:*______	*G:*______		*N:*____ *T:*____	*G:*______
*N:*______	*N:*______		*Tr:*______	*N:*______
*C:*______	*C:*______			*C:*______
*Tr:*______	*Tr:*______			*Tr:*______

Final Tr:____________________

Lesson 32 Quiz

Name______________________________ Date____________

A. Vocabulary & Latin Saying: Give the *principal parts* of the following verbs.

1st	2nd	3rd	4th
cáveo			
gaúdeo			
móveo			
respóndeo			
sédeo			

Latin Saying: I came, I saw, I conquered.______________________________

B. Grammar Questions

1. How do you find the perfect stem?______________________________
2. In Latin grammar, *perfect* means ______________________ and *imperfect* means ______________________.

C. Conjugate the verb **móveo** in the perfect, pluperfect, and future perfect tenses.

principal parts: ______________________________ perf. stem:______________

P	Perfect		Pluperfect	
1				
2				
3				

Future Perfect	

D. Form Drills: Circle tense endings (#1-2) or box any helping verbs (#3-4), parse, then translate.

Prompts Key: ***Cj*** = Conjugation, ***P*** = Person, ***N*** = Number, ***T*** = Tense, ***Tr*** = Translation

1. respondit
*Cj:*_____ *P:* ____ *N:*_____ *T:* ____________
Tr: ______________________________

2. sederamus
*Cj:*_____ *P:* ____ *N:*_____ *T:* ____________
Tr: ______________________________

3. you (p) have taught
*Cj:*_____ *P:* ____ *N:*_____ *T:* ____________
Tr: ______________________________

4. you will have prevented
*Cj:*_____ *P:* ____ *N:*_____ *T:* ____________
Tr: ______________________________

E. Translation: Parse and label, then translate.

KEY: ***C*** = Case, ***Cj*** = Conjugation, ***D*** = Declension, ***G*** = Gender, ***N*** = Number, ***P*** = Person, ***T*** = Tense, ***Tr*** = Translation

1. Fílius | **fructūs** | **bonos** | **ténuit.**

Fílius	fructūs	bonos	ténuit.
*D:*______	*D:*______	*D:*______	*Cj:*____ *P:*____
*G:*______	*G:*______	*G:*______	*N:*____ *T:*____
*N:*______	*N:*______	*N:*______	*Tr:*______
*C:*______	*C:*______	*C:*______	
*Tr:*______	*Tr:*______	*Tr:*______	

Final Tr:________________________

2. Servi | **novi** | **primum** | **adventum** | **víderant.**

Servi	novi	primum	adventum	víderant.
*D:*______	*D:*______	*D:*______	*D:*______	*Cj:*____ *P:*____
*G:*______	*G:*______	*G:*______	*G:*______	*N:*____ *T:*____
*N:*______	*N:*______	*N:*______	*N:*______	*Tr:*______
*C:*______	*C:*______	*C:*______	*C:*______	______
*Tr:*______	*Tr:*______	*Tr:*______	*Tr:*______	

Final Tr:________________________

____

F. Bonus: Parse and label, then translate.

1. One soldier is always the head.

One	soldier	is	always	(the) head.
*D:*______	*D:*______	*Cj:*____ *P:*____	*Tr:*______	*D:*______
*G:*______	*G:*______	*N:*____ *T:*____		*G:*______
*N:*______	*N:*______	*Tr:*______		*N:*______
*C:*______	*C:*______			*C:*______
*Tr:*______	*Tr:*______			*Tr:*______

Final Tr:________________________

Lesson 33 Test: Unit V

Name______________________________ Date____________

A. Vocabulary

Give *all* principal parts.

1. to appear ______________________________
2. to be silent ______________________________
3. to be strong, be well ______________________________
4. to beware of, guard against ______________________________
5. to burn, be on fire ______________________________
6. to fear, be afraid of ______________________________
7. to frighten ______________________________
8. to have ______________________________
9. to hold ______________________________
10. to move ______________________________
11. to order, command ______________________________
12. to owe, ought ______________________________
13. to prevent ______________________________
14. to rejoice ______________________________
15. to remain, stay ______________________________
16. to respond, answer ______________________________
17. to see ______________________________
18. to sit ______________________________
19. to teach ______________________________
20. to warn ______________________________

B. Latin Sayings

1. Cave canem. ______________________________
2. Docēre, delectare, movēre ______________________________
3. Veni, vidi, vici. ______________________________
4. Vídeo et táceo. ______________________________

C. Grammar Questions

1. The stem vowel of the 2nd conjugation is _______________.
2. The infinitive ending for all 2nd conjugation verbs is _________________.
3. Give the regular endings for the principal parts of 2nd conjugation verbs. ______________________

D. Tenses

Using *to move*, give in English the 1st person singular of each tense.

1. present ______________________
2. imperfect ______________________
3. future ______________________
4. perfect ______________________
5. pluperfect ______________________
6. future perfect ______________________

E. Conjugate the verb **hábeo** in all six tenses.

principal parts ____

present stem: ______________________ perfect stem: ______________________

P	Present	
1		
2		
3		
	Imperfect	
1		
2		
3		
	Future	
1		
2		
3		

Perfect	
Pluperfect	
Future Perfect	

F. Form Drills

Circle tense endings (#1-2) or box any helping verbs (#3-4), parse, then translate.

Prompts Key: ***Cj*** = Conjugation, ***P*** = Person, ***N*** = Number, ***T*** = Tense, ***Tr*** = Translation

1. jússerit *Cj:* _____ *P:* _____ *N:* _____ *T:* __________ *Tr:* ______________________	**3.** I had moved *Cj:* _____ *P:* _____ *N:* _____ *T:* __________ *Tr:* ______________________
2. manetis *Cj:* _____ *P:* _____ *N:* _____ *T:* __________ *Tr:* ______________________	**4.** we will rejoice *Cj:* _____ *P:* _____ *N:* _____ *T:* __________ *Tr:* ______________________

G. Translation: Parse and label, then translate.

Key: ***C*** = Case, ***Cj*** = Conjugation, ***D*** = Declension, ***G*** = Gender, ***N*** = Number, ***P*** = Person, ***T*** = Tense, ***Tr*** = Translation

1. Multae	**fácies**	**parvum**	**equum**	**terrúerant.**
*D:*________	*D:*________	*D:*________	*D:*________	*Cj:*____ *P:*____
*G:*________	*G:*________	*G:*________	*G:*________	*N:*____ *T:*____
*N:*________	*N:*________	*N:*________	*N:*________	*Tr:*________
*C:*________	*C:*________	*C:*________	*C:*________	________
*Tr:*________	*Tr:*________	*Tr:*________	*Tr:*________	

Final Tr:____

____

2. Magnus	**portus**	**nomen**	**non**	**hábuit.**
*D:*________	*D:*________	*D:*________	*Tr:*________	*Cj:*____ *P:*____
*G:*________	*G:*________	*G:*________		*N:*____ *T:*____
*N:*________	*N:*________	*N:*________		*Tr:*________
*C:*________	*C:*________	*C:*________		________
*Tr:*________	*Tr:*________	*Tr:*________		

Final Tr:____

____

H. Bonus

The answers will be derivatives of the following Latin words.

appáreo	árdeo	dóceo	gaúdeo

1. Susan, who usually has such good taste, was decked out in a ____________________ outfit.
2. That is a lie that has the ____________________ of truth.
3. Setting a fire in itself is not a crime, but ____________________ is.
4. Tom, who is usually ____________________, was enraged by the accusation.

Lesson 34 Test: Units I, II, & V

Name______________________________ Date____________

A. Vocabulary

Give *dictionary form.*

1. to address ____________________
2. to adore ____________________
3. to ask ____________________
4. to carry ____________________
5. to deny ____________________
6. to fear, be afraid of ____________________
7. to fight ____________________
8. to frighten ____________________
9. to give ____________________
10. to guard, keep ____________________
11. to have ____________________
12. to help ____________________
13. to hold ____________________
14. to judge ____________________
15. to move ____________________
16. to order, command ____________________
17. to overcome, surpass ____________________
18. to prepare ____________________
19. to remain, stay ____________________
20. to report ____________________
21. to respond ____________________
22. to see ____________________
23. to seize ____________________
24. to think ____________________
25. to wait for, expect ____________________

B. Latin Sayings

1. Docēre, delectare, movēre ____________________
2. In umbrā, ígitur, pugnábimus. ____________________
3. nunc aut numquam ____________________
4. semper fidelis ____________________
5. Vídeo et táceo. ____________________

C. Grammar Questions

1. The six attributes of a Latin verb are ______________________________

   ____
2. The forms that provide the stems needed to conjugate a verb in all its tenses are called the

   ______________ ______________.
3. What is the name of the second of these forms? ______________
4. The infinitive of every 1st conjugation verb ends in ______________.
5. The infinitive of every 2nd conjugation verb ends in ______________.
6. The *to be* verb shows ______________, not ______________.
7. Give the English forms of the *to be* verb. ______________________________

   ____
8. The three tenses of the present system are ______________.
9. The three tenses of the perfect system are ______________.
10. In Latin grammar, *perfect* means ______________ and *imperfect* means

    ______________.

D. Tenses: Using *to wash*, give in English the 1st person singular of each tense.

1. present ______________
2. imperfect ______________
3. future ______________
4. perfect ______________
5. pluperfect ______________
6. future perfect ______________

E. Conjugate the verb **amo** in all six tenses.

principal parts ______________________________

present stem: ______________

perfect stem: ______________

P	Present	
1		
2		
3		
	Imperfect	
1		
2		
3		
	Future	
1		
2		
3		

Perfect	
Pluperfect	
Future Perfect	

F. Conjugate the verbs **móneo** and **sum** in the present, imperfect, and future tenses.

principal parts (**móneo**):

____

____

present stem: ____________________

P	Present	
1		
2		
3		
	Imperfect	
1		
2		
3		
	Future	
1		
2		
3		

principal parts (**sum**):

____

____

present stem: ____________________

Present	
Imperfect	
Future	

G. Form Drills

Circle tense endings (#1-2) or box any helping verbs (#3-4), parse, then translate.

Prompts Key: ***Cj*** = Conjugation, ***P*** = Person, ***N*** = Number, ***T*** = Tense, ***Tr*** = Translation

1. culpabit *Cj:* ____ *P:* ____ *N:* ____ *T:* ________ *Tr:* ____________________	**3.** you call *Cj:* ____ *P:* ____ *N:* ____ *T:* ________ *Tr:* ____________________
2. fuistis *Cj:* ____ *P:* ____ *N:* ____ *T:* ________ *Tr:* ____________________	**4.** he does beware of *Cj:* ____ *P:* ____ *N:* ____ *T:* ________ *Tr:* ____________________

H. Translation: Parse and label, then translate.

Key: ***C*** = Case, ***Cj*** = Conjugation, ***D*** = Declension, ***G*** = Gender, ***N*** = Number, ***P*** = Person, ***T*** = Tense, ***Tr*** = Translation

1. **Bella**	**nova**	**spíritum**	**numquam**	**delectaverunt.**
*D:*________	*D:*________	*D:*________	*Tr:*________	*Cj:*____ *P:*____
*G:*________	*G:*________	*G:*________		*N:*____ *T:*____
*N:*________	*N:*________	*N:*________		*Tr:*________
*C:*________	*C:*________	*C:*________		________
*Tr:*________	*Tr:*________	*Tr:*________		

Final Tr:________________________

2. **Dóminum**	**Sanctum**	**voces**	**aeternae**	**laudabant.**
*D:*________	*D:*________	*D:*________	*D:*________	*Cj:*____ *P:*____
*G:*________	*G:*________	*G:*________	*G:*________	*N:*____ *T:*____
*N:*________	*N:*________	*N:*________	*N:*________	*Tr:*________
*C:*________	*C:*________	*C:*________	*C:*________	________
*Tr:*________	*Tr:*________	*Tr:*________	*Tr:*________	

Final Tr:________________________

____

I. Bonus: Parse and label, then translate.

1. **A deep faith does not prevent fears.**

(A) **deep**	**faith**	**does prevent**	**not**	**fears.**
*D:*________	*D:*________	*Cj:*____ *P:*____	*Tr:*________	*D:*________
*G:*________	*G:*________	*N:*____ *T:*____		*G:*________
*N:*________	*N:*________	*Tr:*________		*N:*________
*C:*________	*C:*________			*C:*________
*Tr:*________	*Tr:*________			*Tr:*________

Final Tr:________________________

First Form Latin Final Exam

Name ________________________________ Date _____________

A. Vocabulary: Give *dictionary form.*

Verbs

1. to adore ______________________
2. to address ______________________
3. to ask ______________________
4. to attack ______________________
5. to be strong, be well ______________________
6. to beg, pray ______________________
7. to carry ______________________
8. to disturb ______________________
9. to explore ______________________
10. to fight ______________________
11. to frighten ______________________
12. to greet ______________________
13. to guard, keep ______________________
14. to help ______________________
15. to hold ______________________
16. to move ______________________
17. to order ______________________
18. to prepare ______________________
19. to remain, stay ______________________
20. to sail ______________________
21. to see ______________________
22. to set free ______________________
23. to show, point out ______________________
24. to teach ______________________

Adverbs

1. always ______________________
2. not ______________________
3. now ______________________
4. often ______________________
5. then, at that time ______________________
6. today ______________________

Nouns

1. army ______________________
2. brother ______________________
3. day ______________________
4. earth, land ______________________

Nouns, continued

5. foot ______________________
6. friend ______________________
7. god ______________________
8. harbor ______________________
9. head ______________________
10. house ______________________
11. Italy ______________________
12. kingdom ______________________
13. law ______________________
14. light ______________________
15. lord, master ______________________
16. mother ______________________
17. name ______________________
18. queen ______________________
19. river ______________________
20. sailor ______________________
21. sky, heaven ______________________
22. slave, servant ______________________
23. soldier ______________________
24. son ______________________
25. spirit ______________________
26. thing, matter, affair, business ______________________
27. town ______________________
28. war ______________________
29. world, mankind ______________________
30. year ______________________

Adjectives

1. first ______________________
2. great, large ______________________
3. high, deep ______________________
4. much, many ______________________
5. new ______________________
6. sacred, holy ______________________
7. small ______________________
8. ten ______________________
9. three ______________________
10. wide, broad ______________________

B. Grammar Questions

1. The forms that provide the stems needed to conjugate a verb in all its tenses are called the ______________________ ______________________.
2. What is the name of the second of these forms? ______________________
3. The *to be* verb shows ______________________, not ______________________.
4. In Latin grammar, *perfect* means ______________________ and *imperfect* means ______________________.
5. A complementary infinitive ______________________ the action of the main verb.
6. Verb families are called ______________________ and noun families are called ______________________.
7. Verbs have ______________________ endings and nouns have ______________________ endings.
8. The subject and verb must agree in ______________________ and ______________________ .

9. In Latin, an adjective must agree with its noun in ____________________, ____________________, and ____________________, but not ____________________ .

10. 1st/2nd declension adjectives can modify nouns of the ____________________ declensions.

11. All neuter nouns obey the *neuter rule*:

    The nominative and accusative case forms are ____________________ .

    The nominative and accusative plural case ending is ____________________ .

12. The declension a noun belongs to is determined by the ____________________ ending.

13. A ____________________ follows a linking verb and **renames** the subject.

14. A ____________________ follows a linking verb and **describes** the subject.

15. What is the subject case? ____________________ the direct object case? ____________________

    the indirect object case? ____________________ the possessive case? ____________________

    the *in/by/with/from* case? ____________________ the *to/for* case? ____________________

    the *of* case? ____________________

C. Latin Sayings

1. Anno Dómini (A.D.) ____________________
2. Carpe diem. ____________________
3. Civis Romanus sum. ____________________
4. Pax Romana ____________________
5. Veni, vidi, vici. ____________________

D. Conjugate amo in the present and perfect systems.

principal parts ____________________

present stem: ____________________ perfect stem: ____________________

P	Present	
1		
2		
3		
	Imperfect	
1		
2		
3		
	Future	
1		
2		
3		

Perfect	
Pluperfect	
Future Perfect	

E. Conjugate móneo in the present and perfect systems.

principal parts ______________________________

present stem: ______________________ perfect stem: ______________________

P	Present	
1		
2		
3		
	Imperfect	
1		
2		
3		
	Future	
1		
2		
3		

Perfect	
Pluperfect	
Future Perfect	

F. Conjugate sum in the present system *with meanings.*

principal parts ______________________________

present stem: ______________________

P	LATIN Present	
1		
2		
3		
	Imperfect	
1		
2		
3		
	Future	
1		
2		
3		

ENGLISH MEANINGS Present	
Imperfect	
Future	

G. **Decline** model nouns.

Singular	Plural
mensa	

Singular	Plural
servus	

Singular	Plural
bellum	

Singular	Plural
pater	

Singular	Plural
lex	

Singular	Plural
nomen	

Singular	Plural
portus	

Singular	Plural
res	

H. Form Drills: Noun + Adjective. Parse, then translate in the nominative (#1) or accusative (#2) case.

PROMPTS KEY: ***Cj*** = Conjugation, ***P*** = Person, ***N*** = Number, ***T*** = Tense, ***Tr*** = Translation

1. agni mali

N. *D:* ________ *G:* ______ *N:* _______ *C:* nom.

A. *D:* ________ *G:* ______ *N:* _______ *C:* nom.

Tr: ____

2. Translate **foot**.

D: _________ *G:* __________ *N:* ____________

C: acc. *Tr:* ______________________________

Now translate **second foot**.

____

I. Form Drills: Verbs. Circle tense endings (#1) or box any helping verbs (#3), parse, then translate.

PROMPTS KEY: *Cj* = Conjugation, ***P*** = Person, ***N*** = Number, ***T*** = Tense, ***Tr*** = Translation

1. exspectáverat	2. we have seized
Cj: _____ *P:* ____ *N:* _____ *T:* ___________	*Cj:* _____ *P:* ____ *N:* _____ *T:* ___________
Tr: ______________________________	*Tr:* ______________________________

J. Translation: Parse and label, then translate.

KEY: *C* = Case, ***Cj*** = Conjugation, ***D*** = Declension, ***G*** = Gender, ***N*** = Number, ***P*** = Person, ***T*** = Tense, ***Tr*** = Translation

1. Agrícolae magnam spem cras habebunt.

Agrícolae	magnam	spem	cras	habebunt.
D: ________	*D:* ________	*D:* ________	*Tr:* ________	*Cj:* _____ *P:* _____
G: ________	*G:* ________	*G:* ________		*N:* _____ *T:* _____
N: ________	*N:* ________	*N:* ________		*Tr:* ________
C: ________	*C:* ________	*C:* ________		________
Tr: ________	*Tr:* ________	*Tr:* ________		

Final Tr: ______________________________

____

2. Christus nunc est frater aeternus.

Christus	nunc	est	frater	aeternus.
D: ________	*Tr:* ________	*Cj:* _____ *P:* _____	*D:* ________	*D:* ________
G: ________		*N:* _____ *T:* _____	*G:* ________	*G:* ________
N: ________		*Tr:* ________	*N:* ________	*N:* ________
C: ________			*C:* ________	*C:* ________
Tr: ________			*Tr:* ________	*Tr:* ________

Final Tr: ______________________________

K. Bonus: Parse and label, then translate.

1. The good sisters never have liked to judge.

(The) good	sisters	never	have liked	to judge.
D: ________	*D:* ________	*Tr:* ________	*Cj:* _____ *P:* _____	*Cj:* _____
G: ________	*G:* ________		*N:* _____ *T:* _____	*Tr:* ________
N: ________	*N:* ________		*Tr:* ________	
C: ________	*C:* ________			
Tr: ________	*Tr:* ________			

Final Tr: ______________________________